THE ROSICRUCIFIXION

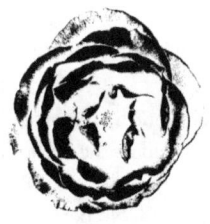

JAKE STRATTON-KENT

HADEAN PRESS

THE ROSICRUCIFIXION
Copyright © 2020 Jake Stratton Kent
Published by Hadean Press
West Yorkshire
www.hadeanpress.com

ISBN 978 1 907881 47 3

Jake Stratton-Kent has asserted his moral right to be identified as the author of this work.

All rights reserved. No portion of this book may be reproduced by any means without the permission in writing of the publisher, except in cases of short passages for purposes of review and citation.

The Rosicrucifixion

Contents

Author's Preamble	9
History vs Heresy	13
Christian Gnostic Sex Magick	25
Venus, the Mother of Heaven	37
The Seven Pillars of Wisdom	45
The Seven Days of Creation	47
Sources and Suppression	51
A Brief Historical Timeline of Christianity	61
The Aeonology of Religious Development	73
Postscript	77

Jesus with His disciples went to the Four Quarters. He gave them commandment each to place their feet by the side of their neighbours'. He prayed and said: 'IOAZAZETH AZAZE ASAZETH, AMEN, AMEN, AMEN EIAZEI EAIZEI KHETH ZAETH ZAETH AMEN, AMEN, AMEN, ABRAZAZAZA BAOZAZZAZ ZAZZOOS AMEN, AMEN, AMEN; AZAAKHAZARAKHA ZARAKHA ZAREATHO ZARBATHOZ ZARAEI ZARAEI AZARAKHA KHARZA BARKHA THAZATH THAZATH, THAZATH, AMEN, AMEN, AMEN. HEAR ME....'

> From the *Gnostic Papyrus*,
> quoted in Florence Farr's
> *Egyptian Magic*.

Author's Preamble

When I use the word 'Christianity', I am not talking about orthodox interpretations of the collection of approved texts comprising the New Testament. I am concerned with the beliefs, practices, and so on of people within particular historical and geographical contexts, whose sacred books and names overlap with Christianity as we now know it. That the most ruthless extermination and censorship was necessary to achieve the distance between these two very different conceptions should not blind us to the reality of the situation, which is that though we are antagonistic to those of the Inquisition, or even of state religion, and sympathetic to their victims, particularly when those victims resemble ourselves, nevertheless the name or costume of the felon is often stolen from the victim. In reality then, the great majority of heretics, Gnostics, and magicians destroyed or opposed by the Roman Church considered themselves to be practising the true form of Christianity. When their practises so closely resemble, or even exceed, those of modern magicians they are worthy of our attention, and no personal religious bias should be allowed to prevent us from exploring this area, or we display the very tendencies we oppose, and continue a process of suppression on behalf of the 'Black Brothers'.

It is a curious fact that the present generation of English occultists seems unable to grasp that there is a concealed interpretation to the Christian scriptures, which the Church itself has lost or suppressed, but which even such books as *Liber 777* would go a long way toward restoring. The idea of treating biblical allegory as occult allegory – even with so crude a weapon as the O.T.O.'s 'secretly interpret everything in terms of the phallus' – seems not to have made much impression on the generality of 'Thelemites'. I once attempted to deal with this subject in a talk whilst under par due to illness and was simply overwhelmed by the wave of incomprehension with which my endeavours were received. No use my asking what the New Testament dove corresponds to in 777... quote: "Jesus was the son of Jehovah" and that was that. Of course, I am an old-fashioned type of occultist with a very specialised vocabulary, whereas younger types may have no idea what a Vesica Piscis is, let alone why it might be connected with Goddess worship. A determined heckler who wants to give a completely different talk simultaneously also doesn't aid comprehension.

Accordingly, I take lance in hand and spur on my charger for a fresh assault on the mountain of conditioning and bullshit that obscures the vision of the assembled multitudes – to free Mankind from the Bonds of the Ancient Sorcery, and get every Brazen Slut in the Hidden Community of Saints ejaculating to the tones of Ave Maria!

To that end, here follows a list of the premises and arguments found within this work:

- The Christians killed by the Romans are not eligible for inclusion in Church martyrology.

- (The Church of) Rome did not bring Christianity to the West.

- Christianity is a combination of sexual occultism, astrology, a variety of pagan cults, and Hellenistic philosophy.

- Much of the New Testament is Gnostic allegory disguised as history.

- The 'Church Fathers' knew there was a hidden interpretation and even hidden books.

- Everything of which witches, heretics, gypsies and Jews have been accused was also said of the early Christians.

- The most important aspects of both contemporary and ancient occultism were central to the Gnostic allegory of which Christianity (and some occult schools) is a sorry remnant.

History vs Heresy

The decline of Hermeticism and Magic in the later Renaissance was due to the eventual success not of persecution but of historical debate. Christian humanists demonstrated convincingly that the Hermetic literature was not older than Moses. The disillusionment attendant upon this (distorted) view of the relative ages of the material was profound. With Hermes no longer the tutor of the oldest biblical sage, the attraction of this 'Wisdom' literature was considerably reduced – persecution merely cleaned up the die-hards who weren't so impressed by the argument. This is not a matter of 'esoteric' interpretation; the reader is directed to the works of serious academics like Frances Yates for amplification. In fact, the Hermeticists were justified in holding to the principle that there was not only a pre-Christian gnosis, but a pre-Christian Christianity. Incidentally, the chief distinction between Hermetic and Gnostic ideas is the nature of the Creator; the Hermeticists hold this Power to be distinct from the First God, as do the Gnostics, but do not make of him an evil demiurge, but an executive power of the Higher God. Much the same relationship may be observed in the relationship between the Kabbalists Ain-Soph, the highest conception of Godhead, and Tetragrammaton, the God of the Four-fold created universe.

> ...secret Gnostic organisations... flourished in various forms during the few centuries immediately before and after the rise of Christianity in the Middle East...
>
> Great stress was laid upon personal mystical experience, to and through which the initiate was guided under conditions of great secrecy...The Gnostics did not confine their studies, or their teachings, to any one religion, but borrowed illustrations from all that were accessible to them. This caused them to be considered Christian heretics, Jews who were trying to undermine Christianity (or) remnants of the Persian sun-worshippers. They have been widely studied by early Christian sages, and it is upon the opinions of these latter that many conclusions have been formed. Little or no investigation of these 'People of Wisdom' has been done by research workers on the spot – in Asia and North Africa – where strong and interesting

traces of their beliefs and practices still remain.' (Arkon Daraul, in *Secret Societies*)

Daraul perhaps might be thought of as a superficial or sensationalist source, so we will have recourse to an authority who – though sensational, was not sensationalist – can never be accused of superficiality. We refer, of course, to one of the most famous modern academics in this sphere, John M. Allegro, whose pioneering work on the Dead Sea Scrolls should have shattered forever the 'historical Jesus' of the Gospels and the Church, were it not for the invincible obstinacy of the Church and the effectiveness of the social conditioning *they* pioneered. That this conditioning should extend to occultists is an intolerable state of affairs, which I shall hopefully rectify.

To this discourse we must add another well-known name, that of John Dee. Allegro held a 'chair' in Semitic languages and literature at Manchester University, and Dee held the Wardenship of Christ's College, Manchester; this connection was compounded by the fact that The Book of Enoch which so inspired Dee, like the Dead Sea Scrolls, was an Essene text. As far as Dee was concerned, the Angels who spoke to Enoch – Uriel and the rest – were the Angels who in turn instructed him. It would not be pushing things too far to point out that Crowley thought

Dee's angels were also involved in his mystical experiences, particularly those described in *The Vision and the Voice*.

Allegro convincingly demonstrates that the Essenes – a kind of mystical faction of Judaism roughly contemporary with the rise of Christianity – were in many respects similar to the Gnostics, a similarity which included an insistence on mystical experience above doctrinal learning. Many occult practises may be traced among these ascetics, including meditation within a circle drawn in the desert. (See the excellent film *The Last Temptation of Jesus Christ*.)

The Book of Enoch, an Essene apocalypse, has strong Babylonian magical themes which are also recognisable in Gnostic texts. The Revelation 'of Saint John' is similar in style and content to these Apocalypses, and also contains Babylonian/Canaanite religious themes in common with other biblical and extra-biblical texts. (Crowley's biographer, John Symonds, derided *The Book of the Law*, on the grounds that it quotes the Revelation once; oddly he seems not to notice that Revelation quotes the Old Testament about ninety times!) The papyrus version of our *Bornless Ritual* originates with a Gnosticising Egyptian; the ritual commences with a rehearsal of the deeds of the god invoked, which on close examination proves to be the Seven Days of Creation, ala Genesis.

This ritual has been described as 'Satanic', and the phallic interpretation put upon it by Crowley would probably be accepted by Allegro (see his *Sacred Mushroom and the Cross*), yet the papyrus is clearly Judaeo-Gnostic in origin, and historically can only be seen as Satanic via the Gnostic identification of Jehovah with Set, Saturn, Satan, *et al*. If we accept this, then of course the Old Testament is Satanic too. As indeed it is, with its compendia of rape, murder, divinely ordained child sacrifice, and genocide. Jehovah advocated race murder long before the same idea occurred to Hitler, and various Gnostics accordingly associated the God of the Old Testament with the Zoroastrian 'devil' Ahrimanes. To these Gnostics there was no possible connection between Jesus and his alleged father.

Allegro's most startling point is the identification of the mythological Jesus with the historical 'Joshua', an Essene put to death on a Tree beneath which he had habitually meditated – and not by the Romans. The Tree motif should remind us of various other dying gods, but also of Buddha, who gained enlightenment under a Tree – a kind of 'dying to the world', rather than dying to save it.

What possible relevance has Buddha in this context? This question is extremely simple to answer, and it is symptomatic of the general ignorance of Christian origins that the question needs answering. Buddhism was originally a mystical revolutionary system, denouncing priestcraft and caste system, and promoting tolerance and mystical attainment – even going so far as to deny the existence or necessity of god, and opposing superstitious observance with a system of transcendental psychology. It is the first historical example of 'humanist religion', as advocated by Huxley *et al*, and undertaken in earnest by Aleister Crowley. Buddhism was founded in approximately 350 BCE, and came into contact with the West via the conquests of Alexander the Great. His successors, particularly the Ptolemaic dynasty of Egypt and the Seleucid dynasty of Syria (which possessed at times an Empire extending to India) retained close links with India, then a Buddhist Empire. Diplomats, scholars, and priests travelled freely between the Hellenistic and Buddhist cultures. Buddhist elements can be traced in great detail both in Gnosticism and the New Testament. This contact was decreased with the contraction of the Seleucid domains, but never fully collapsed, being substantially revived by the later Arab conquests, so that a Buddhist influence on, say, Sufism is not unlikely. Such authors as Holger Kersten (*Jesus Lived in India*, Element Books) take this idea and run with it rather further than I am prepared to follow, but their essential idea is not that unlikely, and even if false has as distinguished a pedigree as the ridiculous claims of the Church, and one of greater antiquity.

It should be remembered that Ptolemaic Egypt was the Greek ruled, multi-racial state in which Alexandria, with its famous library (accidentally singed by Caesar, but utterly destroyed – quite deliberately – by the Christian mob, who also scraped Hypatia to death with oyster shells for the crime of being an intelligent and beautiful woman) was a great centre of Gnosticism, and Syria is also the home of numerous Gnostic and heretical ideas. To this day the 'Old Catholic Church' of Antioch is the source for a great many Gnostic ordinations. Both of these Empires imported elephants and luxury goods from India – and exchanged sages – so the contact was both close and complete. Even after the gradual collapse of these Empires, contact with the West remained. Huge sums of Roman gold have been found in India, and part of the bankruptcy which was to strike Rome under the Caesars was due to profligate consumption of Eastern luxuries.

In later times we find in pseudo-Magriti's *Picatrix* (a notorious compilation of magical texts and practices dating from the Arab Empire) references to a supposed *Book of Buddha*, and much of his material extends back in time to the early Christian period and even earlier (he attributes bronze to Mars in one section, suggesting a period when arms were still made from this metal).

There is no historical difficulty in accepting that Buddhism had an easy route into the intellectual life of the Hellenistic and Roman worlds, and it is easy to see that the convulsions in religion which occurred at this time produced new religions. As Hutton has observed, there were no fanatical pagans to support the Roman state cultus – this may very well have had as much to do with the emergence of a more sophisticated system from the East than with mere dissatisfaction with the old ways in the West among an increasingly educated population. It has been convincingly demonstrated that the idea of an earthly god-man is descended not from Jewish ideas, but from the deification of Alexander and his successors, and their combination with the Buddha figure. Indeed the contact of East and West was two-way, for Buddhism and its art was radically influenced by Hellenistic culture. Statues of Buddha from this time wear Greek drapery, have the solar nimbus behind their heads (where Jesus was to wear his halo) and the impassive expression of the Buddha is that of Alexander, the earthly saviour. This process, which led to the worship of Roman Emperors – the refusal of which civic duty earned Christianity so many alleged martyrs – is part and parcel of the development of the myth of

Christ. The earthly saviour, or Soter, as it is in the Greek, is a title every major dynasty of Hellenised civilisation bore from time to time, along with other supposedly Christian names of god which appear both in the genealogies of the Seleucids and Ptolemies, and in many a Gnostic incantation, and in the pseudo-clerical grimoires of the later Renaissance. The naming of one of these Caesars as 'The Beast 666, the number of A MAN' in the Book of Revelations objects to the deification of human beings and may be readily interpreted as a Gnostic rejection of not Emperor worship alone but of raising any human being to divine status. In this sense, as in others, Jesus and the Beast are one and the same.

Wandering holy-men, such as Jesus is represented to be, were common in the Middle East of the time as has been ably shown in Crowley's work on the subject (*The Gospel according to George Bernard Shaw/Crowley on Christ*), and his teachings have been shown to be less than exceptional in the climate of the time, save for the pro-Roman bias ('render unto Caesar...', etc.), which as Allegro indicates, would have made Jesus an immediate target for a zealot's dagger, were it not a late interpolation. Crowley's work should not be taken as evidence of a historical Jesus however, simply as a demonstration of the ways of the East then and now in order to enhance our understanding.

Crowley himself is unequivocal on this subject. He believed, as I do, that Christianity originated at a time of religious and cultural upheaval and is a combination of many cults and cultures. What it distinctly is *not* is a logical or necessary development of Judaism; it combines elements of many traditions, mainly through the lens of Hellenistic philosophy. The materials from which the canonical Gospels and Epistles are composed is as heterogeneous as the material excluded from the collection in the apocryphal writings and are evidently of the same type despite ruthless (if ignorant and consequently clumsy and inconsistent) editing. It is not stretching the point to say that the gospels are a re-interpretation of Gnostic allegories, planed down and chopped around to appear like a historical narrative. The traditions of Hellenistic literature were widely taught – even to Roman citizens such as Paul – and once taught it is comparatively easy to rewrite existing material in such a style. Indeed much of the Old Testament underwent similar transformations (see the works of Josephus and Philo), and going back to before the Hellenistic period we discover that the 'historical' prophet Daniel can be found in mythological guises both as the object of a hero-cult and as a fallen angel. Indeed the seven-headed beast of the Book of Revelation (whose Gnostic origins are more clearly discernible, lacking as it does the pseudo-historical treatment) may be traced in the cuneiform 'originals' at Ugarit, where Leviathan is identified with 'a wicked city' and as having seven heads (a detail the Old Testament had omitted, preventing the identification before archaeological work at Ugarit, which incidentally also had a Daniel cult). The majority of the material in both the Old and New Testaments can be shown to be an overworking of older material which was never intended to be understood as history, and belonged to radically distinct forms of religious and mystical practice.

The re-interpretation of such material is not necessarily an evil thing. While the traditions of exegesis in use by the Essenes and others frequently wrest new meanings from old forms, the process is one of development rather than censorship and may even be defined as a major part of the role of the mystic within society – uniting Revelation with Tradition. When the object is to distort and suppress, as occurred in the Christian scriptures, the process cannot but hinder truth, and is attended with book-burnings and worse, 'heretic' burning. Even Thelema demands that any interpretation of *The Holy Books of Thelema* be made according to certain principles:

- "each for themselves": No 'official' interpretation is anticipated.

- "The method of science, the aim of religion": Superstitious or inept techniques are disdained as a source of folly and imprecision.

CHRISTIAN GNOSTIC SEX MAGICK

> Crowley found the invocation of the gods very fruitful, and, surprisingly, described it thus: "There's a lot of Jesus force here." It occurred to him that one could invoke Jesus by sexual magic (IX°) as any other god, and why not? "Isn't it a somewhat pedantic and priggish attitude," he wrote, "to invoke all the forces but 'Jesus'? It makes him a kind of 'devil' and so liable to attract all the good people." *The Great Beast*, John Symonds.

In the Essene writings we find the following in *The Rule of the Congregation*:

> And when they are gathered together at the common table to eat and [to drink] new wine, and the communion table is laid out for eating and...drinking, let no man extend his hand over the first-fruits of bread and wine before the Priest (i.e. the Priestly Messiah); for he will bless the first-fruits of bread and wine, and will stretch forth his hand over the bread first. Thereafter, the Messiah of Israel (i.e. the lay Messiah, the Prince) will stretch forth his hand over the bread, and all the Congregation of the

Community [will give blessings], each according to his dignity. It is according to this prescription that they shall proceed at every ritual Meal at which at least ten men are gathered together.

This is the basis and predecessor of the last Supper, and the 'Agapoi' or love feasts of the early Christians, be they Gnostic, Messianist, or whatnot. These first-fruits became identified with the Divine substance itself – which to some Gnostics signified semen and menstrual blood as the most potent earthly vehicles for the Divine Substance, which in its purest form is the LVX of our contemporary occult philosophy. The Last Supper is the origin of our Easter, when Jesus rode into Jerusalem on a donkey and the populace strewed his path with palm leaves – a donkey, almost certainly red in colour, fitting for the beast of Set, as ridden by Dionysus and Priapus in their triumphal processions.

"Dulaure says that apis means high, elevated, powerful, while Pri means principle, first source; therefore Priapus can be translated as the principle of fertility, or first source", so says H. Cutner in *A Short History of Sex Worship*, and of course Priapus, who shares certain titles and feast days with Christ, is a phallic deity:

The phallus there [Egypt] received the greatest honour, as can be seen, for example, from one of the descriptions of a phallic procession given by Herodotus... the great day was March 25 'about our Easter' when a procession in honour of Osiris paraded the towns; and Plutarch tells us that on this representation of their great sun-god three phalli were fastened... Payne Knight insists that the cross in the form of a T served as the emblem of creation and generation before the Church adopted it as a sign of salvation; and Godfrey Higgins was of the same opinion......It is difficult to separate the sun-myth from phallic worship, the two are so closely interrelated. The festivals are almost always in honour of the sun as a fertilising agent...he has triumphed over the powers of darkness (night or water) which sought to deprive him of his virility. This is the symbolic explanation of the various feasts in honour of the sun's resurrection at spring time, no matter under what name or under whose auspices. The resurrection of Jesus Christ is no exception. (Cutner)

The fact that the later Church distorted these elements beyond recognition by all but their initiated opposition is undeniable. However, when modern scientific occultists make such statements as: "It [Christianity] is a denial of birth, death and sex; Jesus Christ was neither properly born nor really died and neither was he a sexual being...", then they are not scientific in the sense of using evidence, nor occultists in the sense of seeking or possessing hidden knowledge. This is simply playing on the ignorance and prejudices of their readers. Surprisingly the same author repeatedly uses the word Gnosis or Gnostic in reference to his own system, despite his apparent ignorance of the sexual meanings of Christian symbols in the Gnostic tradition, which is to say the real significance of those symbols, rather than the orthodox interpretation. It is a curious fact that occult leaders who claim to be scientific seem not to realise that History is also a scientific discipline, perhaps the most useful of all to occultists.

Allegro quotes the account of Epiphianus, a 4th century bishop, regarding such a Gnostic cult interpretation of the same traditional theme:

> The shameless ones have sexual intercourse, and I am truly abashed to say what scandalous things they practise... Following coitus in uninhibited lust,

they proceed to blaspheme Heaven itself. The man and woman take the ejaculated sperm in their hands, step forward, raise their eyes aloft, and with the defilement still on their hands, offer up prayers... They present to Him who is essentially the Father of us all, what lies in their palms, saying, 'We offer unto Thee this gift, the Body of the Messiah.' They then proceed to eat it in their infamous ritual, saying 'This is the Body of Christ, and this is the Pascha (i.e. the Passover Meal) through which our bodies suffer and are made to acknowledge the Passion of Christ.' They behave similarly with a woman's menstrual blood: they collect from her the monthly blood of impurity, take it, eat it in a common meal, and say, 'This is Christ's blood'.

Allegro adds "Like the Essenes, these Gnostics interpreted the biblical visionary's monthly fruiting tree alongside the miraculous stream from the Temple with the Tree of Life, but identified the 'fruit' with female menses". This is borne out in the account of Epiphianus, for he continues: "When they read in the apocryphal writings (Revelation 22.2): 'I saw a tree which bears twelve fruits in a year, and he said to me, 'That is the Tree of Life,' they interpret this allegorically to mean a woman's menstrual discharge".

It is perhaps unnecessarily pedantic of me to point out that its ten branches (the Sephiroth, no less) represent the ten lunations of pregnancy! Nor need I observe with such evident relish that such a pregnancy may conclude in any of the twelve Zodiacal Signs, so that the Woman or Tree contains all of Creation *in potentia* – but I will anyway. Moreover, as "Horapollo, the Alexandrian grammarian, tells us, that the Egyptians when they desire to express the idea of Aeon write 'sun and moon' [the usual symbols for *everlasting*] and when they want to write 'year' they draw 'Isis', that is 'woman'". (*Thrice-Greatest Hermes*, G.R.S. Mead)

Epiphianus is obviously a malicious source, although as Allegro is at pains to point out, the practitioners of these rites were, generally speaking, sincere persons with a wealth of tradition to support their theory and practise. When the bishop goes on to accuse the Phibionite Gnostics of eating children, it is Allegro who points out that "Eating human flesh was a common accusation levelled against Christian groups by outsiders, just as it was against medieval witches. As in similar instances in the Old Testament, where reference is made to fertility rites involving the god Molech, the stories probably derive from a misunderstanding of the word 'seed', which can in many languages, including our own, mean both 'semen' and 'children'". For example, the name of a famous Old Testament figure, Zerubabel, means either: 'Seed' or 'Children' of Babylon/Babalon.

Epiphianus continues:

> When, still in the grip of this frenzy, they reassemble, they smear their hands with their shamefully ejaculated semen and, rising, lift their polluted hands in prayer, standing completely naked, as if thus to demonstrate their sincerity before God. Both men and women pamper their bodies day and night, anointing themselves, bathing, feasting, and sleeping together after indulging in their drinking parties. They despise those who fast, and say that fasting is an offence since it was ordained by the Archon who created the world. One should eat to keep up the body's strength so that it can give of its fruit when required.

This mention of "The Archon who created the world" is significant, since – my fundamentalist heckler aside – the Gnostics generally held that the Creator was evil, and inferior in stature to a conception of God closer to the Ain Soph of the

Kabbalists. By this token of course Jehovah, the Creator-God of the Old Testament, was rejected as the evil one, the chief Archon, so that Christ – the Pure One – could not be identified as his son in Gnostic theology. 'Christ' meant 'the anointed', as in chrism, and the anointing oil represented the Substance of God, either in the form of sexual fluids, or in oils and unguents – frequently psychoactive – which conferred spiritual gifts:

> ...you have been anointed by the Holy One and have knowledge of all things... the anointing which you received from him abides in you, and you have no need that anyone should teach you; as his chrism teaches you about everything, and is true, and is no lie, just as it has taught you, abide in him. (I. John 2.20,27.)

This anointing had a two-fold nature, having the power to bestow gnosis or healing. The tales of Jesus healing with spittle has the same origin, spittle being an acceptable alternative for semen in the local cults of the area. The Rite of Extreme Unction has the same origins. Note the "is true, and is no lie", distinctly reminiscent of the language of the *Emerald Tablet of Hermes Trismigestus* and of the *Leyden Papyrus*, demonstrating again the close correspondence between these Gospels and Gnostico-magical papyri. This anointing with sexual fluids was common in Rome among the various 'Christian' or Gnostic groups, and images of Christ and other Gnostic deities receiving anointing of this kind in ceremonies can be found in the catacombs.

Gnostic cult practice among the Manichaeans (though by no means exclusive to this sect) included the donation of menstrual blood by female members and ritual sex for the procurement of semen: "In return, the Elect offered the women the opportunity to accompany them through the heavenly spheres at each ejaculation uttering the secret names and passwords by which they could pass on to the next stage". In Saint Augustine's attack on the Manichaeans we find more details of such rites, which also connect with the Passover Supper motif: "ground meal was sprinkled underneath the copulating pair to absorb the semen so that it could be mixed and consumed". The Manichaean label was applied fairly indiscriminately by the Church, but the term Catharist was applied to the sect involved in this 'expose', which took place in Carthage. Similar practices were ascribed to the much later heretical movements in the South of France, whose principal sect was known as the Cathars.

The Cathars, whose origins may be traced to Asia Minor and thence to Bulgaria, are only one example of a Gnostic sect surviving to become a heresy when the 'Great Church' ceased to be simply another sect. The Bosnian Moslems for example were only converted to Islam by the Ottomans; prior to this they were an exiled community of Armenian Manichaeans known as the Paulicians, an armed and militant sect, resisting both Islamic and Byzantine pressure in their original home. They were resettled first in Thrace, where they failed to support their Byzantine overlords against the Normans, and then to 'Bosnia'. See Runciman's *Medieval Manichee* for further details on this sect and others which continued after the period in which 'Christian' might equally well mean 'Gnostic sex-magician', after the creed and canonical books were agreed upon by one among many factions – the only one prepared to sacrifice the individualism and freedom of expression that characterises Gnosticism in return for state protection and funding.

One thing most supposed heretical groups agreed upon was the unreality of the crucifixion, which is curious since it is directly involved in the symbolism of the Love Feast. The blood and water which flowed from Christ's wounds were also identified with the fruit of the Tree of Life, and the careful reader will note that these would be taken to represent menses and semen, making Christ's sexuality somewhat ambivalent in this context at least. It is also worth noting that the Gnostics observed the movements of Sun AND Moon and connected their waxing and waning to reflect the ebbing and flowing of the Divine Substance; their sexual doctrines were accordingly egalitarian, and their rites frequently involved the 'worship' of the luminaries. This may well connect with both Islamic and Thelemic ritual practice.

> The Manichaeans honour the sun and moon, but 'not as deities, rather as channels through which one may attain to God...They offer prayers to the sun during the day, according to its position in the sky, and to the moon at night, when it is visible; should it fail to appear, they stand in a posture of prayer, facing the north, on the setting sun's path of return to the east. (Runciman)

In the combination of sexual and solar worship we are reminded of certain Egyptian legends regarding apes, observed to adore the sun while in a state of erection at sunrise. We have already referred to Horapollo of Alexandria interpreting Egyptian hieroglyphs of Sun and Moon as the idea of 'Aeon' or 'everlasting', while 'Isis', or 'woman' meant Year. The Zodiac as a map of the body of Isis, and the 'cycle' of woman, is the basic model for real understanding of much ancient occult thought.

In considering the role of the motions of the heavenly bodies in cult practise it is instructive to consider Babylonian mythology. In this schema, which is found throughout the ancient Near and Middle East, the planet Venus is accorded a unique part; alongside the sun and moon it is considered as superior to the other planets and stars. This is a prefiguring of the Christian trinity. This status is retained, and accordingly developed, in the proliferation of Gnostic cults of the period.

Venus, the Mother of Heaven

The historicisation of the myth cycle of the Gnostic redeemer was a central part of the rise of the Great Church, and has, through a process of suppression and censorship, completely obscured the real nature of the varied factions of the Gnostic and Messianist movements. On closer examination however it is possible to recognise certain features of the approved and historicised myth and the remaining heretical legends. The prime candidate for such comparison is in the legend of Simon Magus and his consort Helen of Tyre, which has many features in common with the myth of Jesus and Mary Magdalen, which was originally of the same type.

This Gnostic myth-cycle was sufficiently popular as to require special action by the Church. Accordingly, the Gospels give accounts of Simon's 'conversion' (a situation equivalent to Osiris becoming a member of an Adonis cult!). Not only is Simon historicised in his turn but given a villain's role nearly equal to that of Judas (who may simply have been the military Messiah as Jesus was the spiritual). But it is in his companion, Helen, that we must seek the gnosis, for she is none other than the Gnostic (and Orthodox) Sophia. Her alternative name, Achamoth, is directly related to Chokmah, and as the first departure from the Pleroma She is also equivalent to the Curse of the Grade, invoked by the duality of Chokmah. Her fall through successive incarnations, in the legend of Simon Magus, ends with him discovering her in a Tyrian brothel. We should remember that sacred prostitution formed a part of the cult of Melqart and Astarte in Tyre, and also that Church tradition makes Magdalen a prostitute. Simon convinced her that he was the First God (not the Archonic Creator) and She his First Thought; she was also Helen of Troy and so on. Her fall had necessitated His own descent to rescue her, and to show *those who could hear* how to return to the Fullness or Pleroma. This was achieved by gnosis, through one's own efforts, and once in this blessed state one was no longer subject to the Law (the old doctrine - this period corresponds pretty much with the turn of the Aeon, much as the reception of *Liber AL* did). Incidentally Crowley had a memory of an incarnation as a prostitute named Astarte saved from the brothel by a priest and employed subsequently as a Temple prostitute!

It is significant that Mary Magdalen is not referred to as a prostitute in any of the Gospels, despite the strength of popular tradition claiming this was her occupation prior to her becoming a follower of Jesus. Luke describes her as a woman "out of whom went seven devils", and in *The Holy Blood and the Holy Grail* the authors suggest this may have more connection with "The cult of Ishtar or Astarte – the Mother Goddess and 'Queen of Heaven' – (which) involved...a seven-stage initiation. Prior to her affiliation with Jesus, the Magdalene may well have been associated with such a cult. Migdal, or Magdala, was the 'Village of Doves', and there is some evidence that sacrificial doves were in fact bred there. And the dove was the sacred symbol of Astarte." Of course, Astarte just happens to be the name of the Queen in whose territory Isis finds Osiris' body.

> The mysteries of Isis, holy, venerable, and not to be disclosed to the uninitiated... are nothing else than the robbing of the member of Osiris, and its being sought for by the seven-robed and black mantled Goddess...having round her, nay robing herself in seven aetheric vestures – for thus they allegorically designate the planet-stars, calling (their spheres) aetheric vestures. (Mead)

These seven vestures are also the 'Seven Veils' removed by Salome at the sacrificial decapitation (or castration?) of John the Baptist (or Pillar) in her dance. The probability of a connection here with the cult of Cybele and with her eunuch priests is hard to deny. It is interesting to note that at least one major sect of Gnostics, the Naasenes, were closely associated with this cult, but practised sexual abstinence rather than castration. That this abstinence may have been periodically, and ritually, abandoned is more than likely. Again there is the Gnostico-Hermetic tradition regarding the Seven Archons, whose astrological contributions to the psychic constitution of the incarnating human were also 'veils' of the original 'spark' of the divine fire. Particularly among the Gnostics these archons were the attendants of the demiurge, perceived as evil due to the materiality of his creation. These are accordingly identified with seven devils. This concept must be of extremely ancient vintage, since Sumero-Akkadian magical texts also refer to the 'seven devils'. In this case of course Magdalen has been 'purified' of the influence of these devils, or transcended what might be termed her personal astrological karma. This makes the Jesus character a Gnostic or hermetic exorcist – a traditional middle-eastern magician-hero. It is worth comparing these seven devils with the "Seven vultures of unrighteousness" in *Liber B vel Magi*. Thelema is not Gnostic in the traditional world-hating sense, but the themes running through the Gnostic texts are paralleled by Hermetic texts and traditions; the main distinction between them is their attitude to the creation. With the Hermeticists (and probably among the Harpocratian 'Gnostics'), the Creation is not perceived in the same light, though many of the characters or roles and the storylines are closely linked. Both the 'Egypto-Christian Qaballism' of the Golden Dawn and the Thelemic cosmology are also within this tradition, the former as a synthesis of the best Old-Aeon schools, the latter both a rediscovery of the pristine original sense of these themes and a major development upon the synthesis.

The authors of *The Holy Blood and the Holy Grail* go on to describe an un-named woman who appears one chapter before this first mention of the Magdalen, who ANOINTS Jesus with precious ointments. Again, popular tradition associates this woman with the Magdalen. Strenuous attempts were made to tarnish this important figure in the drastically edited and demonstrably altered texts. The so-called *Secret Gospel of Origen* is in fact a more complete version of St. Mark's Gospel, which prompted the Church Father Origen to remark "not all true things are to be told to all men". Despite these efforts Magdalen is one of the major figures in the Jesus legends; he accords her every respect throughout "in a unique and preferential manner". These authors theorise that Jesus did not die at the crucifixion, but was already married to Magdalen, and either survived the crucifixion somehow, noting the possibility that it was a mystery ritual, and went on to found a bloodline. These arguments, whilst we need not take them literally, reflect a whole genre of Gnostic ideas about the crucifixion, and the book is worthy of closer examination. Jesus and Magdalen, Simon and Helen – where do these adapted legends come from?

> Celsus (A.D. 150-75) knew of groups of Harpocratians – that is, worshippers of Horus – some of whom derived their traditions from Salome, others from [Miriam], and others again from Martha (Origen. *Contra-Celsum*, v.62). This suggests an Egyptian setting. For Salome, and Maria or Miriam, the Sisters of Jesus, see *Did Jesus Live 100 BC* 405 f.; for Martha, Our Lady, see ibid. 375 ff). In the Gnostic 'Acts of Philip', [Miriam] is the 'virgin sister of Philip, and plays an important role as prophetess. She is to Philip as Thekla to Paul, or Helen to Simon. Compare with this the 'sister wife' whom Paul demands the right to take about like 'the rest of the Apostles and the Brethren of the Lord and Cephas' (I.Cor.ix.5; DJL, 229). Salmon...

refers to the Mary (Magdalen) of the 'Pistis Sophia', the chief questioner of the Master and His favourite disciple, the sister of Martha. (Mead)

King tells us that "Simon Magus, who passed himself off upon the Samaritans as the *third* manifestation of Christ, was worshipped...in statues made in the form of Jupiter. His famous concubine Helena...was similarly adored under the forms of Minerva and the Moon."

THE SEVEN PILLARS OF WISDOM

Simon is called 'The Pillar' in Gnostic literature, also 'the Standing One', and this title was also used for leaders of the Christian community in Jerusalem (Galatians 2.9.). The uses of the symbol of the Pillar in the scriptures are extensive and enlightening: Moses and his people were led by a pillar of fire by night and a pillar of smoke by day; God speaks in a pillar of cloud; in the apocryphal book Ecclesiasticus 24.4 we find "In the high places did I fix my abode, and my throne was in the pillar of cloud"; and in the *Wisdom of Solomon* the feminine Wisdom is identified with the pillars:

> she became unto them a covering in the daytime, and a flame (light) of stars through the night...

In the book of Proverbs 9.1. She is described as having "Built her house, she has set up her seven pillars". These pillars are the Days of Creation, with their planetary associations, since She, as the Morning Star, is the herald of all seven.

The Seven Days of Creation

Compare Genesis. Chapter 1:1: "In the beginning God created the heaven and the earth", with the *Bornless Rite*: "Ye I invoke, the Bornless One; Thee that didst create the Earth and the Heavens". The direct comparison of the opening of the ritual continues right through Genesis 1:31. to Genesis 2:2. Additionally, many of the titles and godnames used throughout the ritual make explicit its associations with Set-Typhon. In short, Set is credited with being the creator god, responsible for events on the Seven Days of Creation.

The Seven Days of Creation are a recurring theme in many Gnostic texts, and the astrological connotations of verse 14 point to a very different kind of cultus from the orthodox Judaeo-Christian. The "Spirit of God" of verse 2, even in the English, sounds suspiciously like a distinct personality from 'God'. Is this the 'Wisdom' Goddess who is set over the Pillars of Wisdom? Bear in mind that virtually every Hebrew angelic name means 'such and such of God'.

A Hebrew title of Venus is 'Pillar of the Dawn'. Babylonian kings were identified with the Morning Star, and Hebrew King-Messiah's anointed beneath a pillar (plausibly one pillar of Solomon for the spiritual Messiah, and the other pillar for the military Messiah). In Revelation 22:16. it is Jesus who is the "bright Morning-star"; in the Mystery Cults of Greece the same title is bestowed upon Iacchus, the reborn Dionysus (the links between the legends of Jesus and Dionysus are extensive – both ride in triumph on an ass, one is tried by Pontius, the other by Pentheus, and so on). If this star/pillar had led the Israelites through the desert, how much the more relevant that it should be associated with divinely appointed leader figures! Furthermore the whole concept of baptism is thrown into confusion when we realise that the word for 'dip, baptise' is also the word for 'stand, pillar', so that John the Baptist – by the kind of wordplay beloved by the Gnostics – was also John the Pillar, and it is whilst visiting him that Jesus received the Holy Spirit in the form of a dove, emblem of Venus. Allegro speculates as to the significance of the dawn meditations of the Essenes and other sects: were they strictly solar, or had they a double significance with the association with the Morning-star? As their leaders were all 'Pillars' it seems more than likely. The stone or pillar is also an extremely ancient Egyptian symbol, connected with Set, and occurs also in the cultus of the Yezidi, again along with sevenfold motifs attached. In the case of the Yezidi it is worth mentioning that one name for Venus was Lucifer, the Light-bringer. The dew associated with the dawn was seen as associated with Venus and the anointing ceremonies aforementioned. Alchemical processes are still performed with dew, and it is significant that the healing properties associated with dew can be traced back to Gnostic practise, and thence back to earlier Hellenistic and Eastern cults. This dew was quite unequivocally associated with the Divine Substance, manna, semen.

> The name Mary (the name given to the mother of Jesus and to many other women in the Gospels) is curiously like Myrrha, the mother of Adonis. Lempriere says that at the birth of her son (the father was Cynyras, King of Cyprus, her own father) she fled into Arabia and was changed into a tree called myrrh. Mary is the Greek form of the Hebrew 'Mir-yam', the name of the sister of Moses, who was, according to one legend, the mother of Joshua, which word means, like Jesus, the Saviour. The meaning behind Miriam is 'bitter', but the word may also have come from myrrh or 'mare', the sea. Robert Taylor says it was one of the names of

the Goddess Venus, called the Marine Venus by the Romans, and the Venus Anadyomene, the Venus rising out of the sea, by the Greeks. (Cutner)

To the Gnostics there was absolutely no distinction between Isis, Mary (Virgin and Magdalen are only aspects of each other), Helen of Tyre, and Astarte. Whether she was seen as Lunar or Venusian depended not on differences of doctrine but on context; similarly, Jesus seems able to represent both Venus and the Sun or even both simultaneously, as with the water AND blood issuing from his side.

SOURCES AND SUPPRESSION

Until the discovery of the Nag Hammadi library we possessed less documents from the Gnostics describing their practices and beliefs than hostile exposes. Among the most useful, but also the most vitriolic, of these is the *Treatise of Iranaeus of Lugdunum against the Heresies*. It is this author to whom Kenneth Grant somewhat sloppily refers as a "Gnostic writer". This second century bishop was instrumental in the gradual process of winning over the Romans. His method was simple: teach the Romans to distinguish his Church from the various Gnostic sects. The title 'Christians', meaning simply 'anointed ones', was not invented by the Church, but was a term the Romans used to describe a proliferation of Gnostic and messianic sects, some of whom may have regarded the Jesus legends as superior or equal to the Simon stories, all of whom practised rites identifiable as belonging to one genre, matters of detail apart. Some of his attacks are crude and unworthy of the average *Sun* journalist (for example, replacing the names of a series of Gnostic emanations with the names of vegetables); his methods include about every 'unfair persuasive technique' known to advertising executives and politicians. However, he also provides a quantity of quotations and bowdlerised 'reconstructions'. His 'irony' has appealed to equally self-assured clergymen for some centuries, content that when the Romans ceased persecuting 'the Great Church' they were able to combine forces against the 'heretics' thus created.

Iranaeus' account (and that of his commentator and editor F. R. Montgomery Hitchcock) of the Gnostic system of Valentinian is of particular interest. Although many similar systems existed among these related sects, Valentinian's system "was the most popular and imaginative", and accordingly seems to have influenced a variety of sects, to whom the ideas involved were in any case familiar.

> Starting with the idea that matter was evil, and that, therefore, the Father, the supreme Unknown and transcendent Deity, who is described as Bythus, Proarche, or Propator, had no part in the creation, these Gnostics filled up the void with a graduated scale of intermediaries, acting in pairs, and divided into groups of ogdoads, decads, and dodecads, which they called agencies or aeons or emanations. These were all produced

from the Supreme God, collectively made up the number thirty, and constituted the Pleroma. This system...was borrowed from Pythagorus, Plato, Democritus... also based, to a large extent, upon the three Egyptian enneads or cycles of Gods in which the Deity was supposed to manifest Itself....The Supreme God of the Gnostics became identified with the Pleroma or fullness, which consisted of a number of created divinities. The most important of these is Nous or Monogenes (only begotten or first born), who alone has knowledge of the Supreme God, and who leads others to that knowledge...a solitary aeon called Stauros (cross) or Horos (boundary) is employed in keeping each aeon in its place. Of this aeon Neander (*Church History*, II.73) remarks: 'it is a profound idea of the Valentinian system that as all existence has its ground in the self-limitation of Bythus, so the existence of all created beings depends on limitation'. (Iraneaus)

It is interesting to observe that the planet Mars, and the month of the old Roman calendar which is primarily ruled by that planet, have their etymological root in the word 'Margo', meaning 'extremity, limit, edge, mark, boundary, border or attainment'. And of course the Egyptian Horus (Horos) was linked to Mars by the ancient syncretists.

Horos, the boundary, is also called Redeemer and Saviour in Valentinian's system. It is also the cross separating, and is said to be described in the text:

> I am not come to bring peace but a sword (Matt.x.34). The services of Horos were requisitioned for Sophia, the last of the aeons, who in her eagerness to see the light of the Supreme God, which could only be seen with safety by the first mystery, moved out of the Pleroma into the 'void' and was brought back by Horos. But from her wanderings outside the Pleroma the world and mankind originated. For the fall of the errant aeon into matter resulted in the quickening of a shapeless thing called Achamoth (Hebrew, hokhmoth, plural of hokhmah, wisdom the second of the Hebrew Sephiroth)...Seeing and pitying the struggles of Achamoth to reach the light, Christ touched her with his Cross and she became the soul of the world. (Iraneaus)

This title is recognisable in the Renaissance occultist's term: 'Anima Mundi', referring to Isis, after the Hermetic texts had re-appeared in the West. The Horos/Sophia and Christ/Achamoth stories are obviously parallel. In addition, we may see many correspondences between this lore and that of the Kabbalah and the so-called *Chaldean Oracles*. Although the Pleroma did not suit Crowley's conception of the gods (see *Commentaries of AL*), the ancient counterparts of Crowley's "Wrong of the Beginning (*Liber LXV*) and other Gnostic ideas are sufficient to enable us the relate to the Class A documents as similar, and related to, the Gnostic and 'Christian' texts, in origin, content and mode of interpretation.

King, in his *Gnostics and their Remains*, speaks of the curious Gnostic gems, saying "the figures are for the most part drawn from the ancient iconography of the Egyptian religion...adopted... by the newly arisen sects, holding the doctrines of Christianity strangely amalgamated with the old teachings of the Mysteries". He goes on to say that of these symbols "the most frequent and most important is the Jackal-headed Anubis... bearing the caduceus of Hermes to denote his office of conducting souls, not as of yore through the shades of the lower world, but along the planetary path to their final rest in the Pleroma". King relates that Anubis is frequently depicted as "weigher of souls" in scenes drawn from Egyptian iconography, and "in [this] character he stands here for Christ...but his successor in medieval art is the Archangel Michael, who holds the scales". He also equates images of Hermes drawing souls out of the underworld with identical images of Christ in medieval icons, and draws the obvious conclusion that the images of Hermes inspired the later version. He notes further that the Zoroastrian Hell was not one of eternal punishment, but a purifying fire obtaining "restoration of their pristine state". Origen, who we met earlier in this work, was among those early Christians who subscribed to this 'heretical' doctrine. The Persian Zoroastrians influenced the Hebrews; indeed it has been said that the word 'Pharisee' means Persian, and Zoroastrians are indeed known as Parsees to this day. The word Kether comes from a Persian original Kataris meaning *crown*, and of course Alexander's world empire, which made this religious revolution possible, indeed inevitable, was built upon the conquered Empire of the Persians, who had previously held territory in Egypt and India as Alexander was to do.

King writing in 1864 is somewhat coy in his next section, where he refers to the Naasenes or Ophites: "They interpreted Hermes' leading souls through darkness into Elysium as Christ's guiding the minds of the *enlightened* out of *Ignorance* into *Knowledge*, in their spiritual sense of the words. As may well be supposed, they descanted largely upon that peculiar symbol, under which Hermes, surnamed Cyllenius, was worshipped". He refers to the phallic 'Herm' which represents Hermes as guide of the dead, "exactly as the same figure, lingam, represents Siva, Lord of the dead in modern Hinduism". He then adds that this phallic attribute, standing for the guide of the dead, was the earliest kind of gravestone, not only in the East, but, imported from Asia Minor into Rome, it "regularly surmounted the door of the sepulchre". I have studied a key text originating with this sect, in which the Hermetic Phallus, and a form of sexual gnosis, are discussed in great detail; their ideas are, as King rightly and discreetly says "supported by ingenious applications of the symbolism employed in the Eleusian, Phrygian, and Samothracian Mysteries". As we have seen, it is not only Gnosticism that thus combined traditions into a grand scheme, as Crowley says in his introduction to Levi's *Key to the Mysteries*: "There is no single feature in Christianity which has not been taken bodily from the worship of Isis, or of Mithras, or of Bacchus, or of Adonis, or of Osiris".

King draws attention to the "drawing, the discovery of which created such a sensation at Rome a few years back, scratched (*graffito*) roughly on the plaster of a room in a house buried (in ancient times) under the extended buildings of the Palatine. It represents this same jackal headed man holding in front of him a Latin cross with his outstretched hands, and standing on a pedestal, in front of his worshipper, who makes the customary form of *adoration* by raising his hand to his lips, and who has expressed the object of his handiwork by the inscription 'Alaxemenos worships his God'. The production of some devout, but illiterate Gnostic, it is construed by its present owners into a shocking heathen blasphemy, and a jibe upon the good Christian Alaxemenos, because they mistake the jackal's head for that of an ass, and consequently imagine an intentional caricature of their own Crucifix." The present owners are of course the Vatican authorities, and their 'mistake' is in fact a deliberate distortion, in the tradition of Iranaeus, Hippolytus and the rest of the gutter-press saints.

The sign made by raising the hand to the lips cannot but be the 'Sign of Silence'. Possibly Alaxemenos was of the sect called 'Harpocratians'; in any case Harpocrates' association with Silence and Secrecy is a Gnostic interpretation, and "[Gnostic images of] *Harpocrates* or *Horus* (the vernal Sun), having the symbol of fecundity monstrously exaggerated and seated upon a lotus" are the subject of another of King's illuminating asides. He says of Harpocrates, or rather Hoor-Paar-Kraat, that "He often appears accompanied by Anubis in the character of his messenger". This is somewhat reminiscent of the passage in *The Book of the Law* where we read "It is revealed by Aiwass, the minister of Hoor-Paar-Kraat". Many of the Invocations in the *Leyden Papyrus*, close relatives of the *Bornless Rite*, are addressed to Horus, and to his messenger Anubis. In the word play typical of this period, Horoscope (meaning originally the Sign in the Ascendant) was linked with Horus as Lord of the Hour, reflecting the importance of Horus and Anubis, his messenger, in the magical papyri.

A Brief Historical Timeline of Christianity

Prehistory: the prophetic movement within Jewish/Canaanite religion. The minority monotheism of the prophets involved a conception of Jehovah as sole supreme deity. Alongside this coexisted cults from which the conception of Jehovah had been evolved; consequently more 'primitive' and pagan conceptions of Jehovah existed among the great majority. In these Jehovah is indistinguishable from many and various regional Baals, associated with mountains and thunder and sexual potency, and partnered with a female deity particularly execrated by the prophets but hugely popular with the people. She was known as Astarte, Ishtar, or 'Astaroth', the latter perhaps an insulting prophetic pun on her real name; Astaroth means 'crowds', the play on words suggests an elitist minority's impatience with the religion of the masses.

> Babylonian religious ideas…came westward through the medium of myths, some fragments of which have actually been found among the Amerna tablets… an explanation of the remarkable

resemblance between certain of the early narratives of Genesis and the stories dealing with similar subjects (e.g. Creation and Deluge) which have been found in Babylonia. We may suppose that these stories had long been known to the Canaanites, and that the Hebrews, after their entry into Palestine, gradually adopted them, as they adopted many other elements of the Canaanitish civilisation. (Bedale, in *Peake's Commentary on the Bible*)

The emergence of the Messianist movement is then largely the result of the prophetic movement's importance as a nationalist force. Terrific persecutions and massacres of Canaanite religious groups characterise the activities of the prophets and their champions.

But though the religion of Yahweh was officially recognised by royal authority, the Canaanite cults continued in both kingdoms [Judah and Israel. Ed.] side by side with it. Asa made an attempt to put a stop to some of its worst features in Judah by removing many of the kedeshim (EV. 'sodomites') [a species of male sacred prostitute, the name comes from

Qadosh, holy. Ed.], persons dedicated to immorality in connexion with the cult of the Baalim, and destroying many of the Canaanite images, including 'an abominable image for Asherah' erected by the queen-mother Maacah, whom he deposed from her official position. And Jehosophat continued his efforts, removing kedeshim, who still remained in the country...Elijah...managed to bring over the populace to his side, so that they slaughtered many of the Baal priest-prophets...Jehu went far to stamp out the Tyrian worship by a series of massacres... Jezebel, at his orders was thrown from the window of the palace...having thus nearly wiped out both the royal houses, he summoned all the priests and worshippers of Baal as though for a sacrifice to their god, and ruthlessly massacred them all in their temple. (Bedale, in *Peake's Commentary on the Bible*)

Much of this activity centred around the establishment of the Jerusalem Temple as the sole place of worship. This measure was to prevent the worship of Jehovah being contaminated by 'lesser conceptions' (from whom of course the sanitised Jehovah was derived):

> Josiah at once led the way in a wholesale destruction of objects connected with pagan worship; and with these were included many of the sanctuaries in which Yahweh had been worshipped in what was then understood to be an unworthy and primitive manner, the rites being scarcely distinguishable in the popular mind from those of the Canaanites. (Bedale, in *Peake's Commentary on the Bible*)

A full description of the events leading up to the martyrdom of the Essene Messiah, Joshua, the role of Messianist movements and their relations with Gnostic schools and the early Christian movement is outside the scope of this treatise. We wholeheartedly recommend Prof. Allegro's *The Dead Sea Scrolls and the Christian Myth* for an examination of this contentious area. That this historical figure was already identified with the Messiah, even if as a foreshadowing, is a matter of historical record; that he died horribly upon a tree is also demonstrable. He is not remotely connected with the Jesus stories of the Gospels, except inasmuch as he forms the link between the Messiah figure and the dying god of Canaanite (and other forms of) paganism. The lens of Gnostic thought elevated the pagan conception to a higher conception of Godhead – much as the Jews had attempted to do in 'improving' their local cults. The only failure of Gnosticism in this department was its tolerance and variety, as compared with ruthless missionary zeal.

The Christian Church is a misconception historically. Saints Barnabas and Paul are credited with the historic break with the Jewish religion, declaring the rites of that religion to be unnecessary for entry into 'the Christian Church' – a declaration which made possible a completely alien interpretation of the existing literature and folklore for a gentile audience. This is often referred to as the beginning of the Church of Paul; it is not a continuation of early Christianity, nor was it the sole form of western Christian movement, as Gnosticism and the mystery cults were also moving throughout the Roman Empire, including various sects interpreting essentially the same material. "For the first few centuries the Church was not much more than a spasmodically persecuted minority", says *Hutchinson's Encyclopaedia*. This period includes:

177 AD: the approximate date of Iranaeus' elevation to Bishop of Gaul and authorship of *Against the Heresies*. At the time there were already Christian-Gnostic movements in Gaul. Hutchinson's agrees with the generality of historians that "in the 3rd century more determined attempts to destroy it [Christianity]

were made under Severus, Decius, and Diocletion. Toleration was obtained by Constantine's victory at Milvian Bridge outside Rome (312), and Christianity became the established religion of the Roman Empire". Or so it appears, but what form of Christianity did Constantine mean? Thus says *Lempriere's Classical Dictionary*: "Constantine has been distinguished for personal courage, and liberally praised for the protection which he extended to the Christians. Though he at first persecuted the Arians, he afterwards inclined to their opinions and favoured their cause". Rome accordingly recognised and protected Paul's Church, and was initially happy to persecute the rival Arian Church. Who was Arius and what did his followers believe?

> ...a system of Christian theology which denied the complete divinity of Christ. It was founded c. 310 by Arius, and condemned as heretical at the Council of Nicea in 325 AD. Some 17th and 18th century theologians held Arian views akin to those of modern Unitarianism (that God is a single being, and that there is no such thing as the Trinity'. (*Hutchinson's Encyclopaedia*)

This seems like a return to Judaic monotheism, and an inevitable intellectual reaction to the historicisation of the Jesus-legends. As indeed was Nestorian Christianity, founded by Nestorius (died c. 457 AD), whose creed denied divine status to Mary as the mother of the man Jesus, not the divine Christ. Gnostic influences, and a rational response to the historicisation process can account for the majority of later heresies. *Hutchinson's* details other respectable contenders for the title of true Church: "Montanism, a 'movement within the early Church which strove to return to the purity of primitive Christianity. Originating in Phrygia in about 156 (prior to Iranaeus' 'historical Jesus theology') with the teaching of a prophet named Montanus, it spread to Asia Minor, Rome, Carthage and Gaul. The Emperor Tertullian [155-222 AD, long prior to Constantine, and contemporary with Iranaeus,] Carthaginian father of the Church, the first important Christian writer in Latin; became a Montanist in 213". Iranaeus' claim to recognition as a saint rather than a mere propagandist resides in his plea for 'clemency' for these same Montanists when 'Christian' persecution descended on them. Their only crime was thinking for themselves, and it was Iranaeus' work that defined such 'thought-crimes'. Doubtless he 'meant well'.

On Gnosticism *Hutchinson's* is equally concise: "esoteric cult of Divine Knowledge (a synthesis of Christianity, Greek philosophy, Hinduism, Buddhism, and the mystery cults of the Mediterranean) which was a rival to early Christianity...It influenced the development of Christianity; and the French Cathars and the modern Mandeans in South Iraq descend from it". *Hutchinson's* says the clash with the Church came in the 4th century, as with Montanism. Up until this point any one of these movements could claim with equal voice to be the authentic teaching. As we have seen, the support of Emperors is a fickle thing; at least two of the most important figures seem to have gone off 'Pauline Christianity' and sought the truth in purer and less irrational movements, both on the Eastern side of the Middle Ocean, where sources were less westernised.

If the Church lacked sufficient support until the 4th century to establish its claims to orthodoxy then obviously any Christian martyrs prior to this period could well have been Montanists, Arians, or Gnostic sex-magicians. They are less likely to have been Paulinists, as these seem to have been the authors of the 'render unto Caesar' forgeries, and could have weaselled their way out of undesirable state attention more readily than could a genuine prophesying teacher, opposed to private property, caste system and the worship of deified human beings (Jewish or Roman!). With one or two adjustments *Hutchinson's* description of Gnosticism could apply equally well to Saint Paul's Christianity: "a synthesis of primitive Christianity/Messianism, Greek philosophy, eastern religion and the mystery cults of the Mediterranean. Influenced the development of Gnosticism and Kabbalah, the Franco-Italian Imperial Churches were descended from it".

As we have seen, Iranaeus' mission took place in Gaul, already home to Arian, Montanist, and Gnostic 'Churches', sufficiently deep-rooted to re-emerge in the Middle-Ages as part of Catharism. Many early Kabbalistic writings, such as the Bahir, were also written in Southern 'Gaul'. The Visigoths who settled Gaul in late Roman times were Arian Christians and had Arian bishops. Constantine, the supposed founder of Roman Catholicism in popular legend, also became more sympathetic to the Arians. Gaul was pivotal to the spread of the 'Holy Roman Empire', which cannot in fact be ascribed to Constantine at all, but to the much later Clovis, who was not 'Emperor of Rome' but King of the Franks.

> Clovis, the first Christian King of the Franks, was an ambitious and powerful monarch. His name was properly written Chlodwig, which was shortened to

Ludwig, the German form, and finally softened to Louis, the present French form. He was a son of King Childeric and his queen, Basina, and was born about 466 CE. The Franks were then pagans, and Clovis was educated as an idolater. In 481 CE he succeeded his father, who reigned over the Salian tribe. That kingdom was then limited to the island of the Batavians, or the marshes at the mouth of the Rhine, with the ancient dioceses of Tournay and Arras... his dominions were soon extended by bloody conquest, including 'the Belgic cities' and 'the ample diocese of Tongres, which Clovis subdued in the tenth year of his reign.' In 493 he married Clotilda, a Christian princess, a daughter of Chilperic, King of Burgundy. She persuaded him to profess her religion, and he avowed his conversion in 496. His subjects also then changed their religion, and burned the idols which they had formerly adored. (J. Michelet, in *Spofford's Library of Historical Characters and Famous Events*)

According to Gibbon however, "His ambitious reign was a perpetual violation of moral and Christian duties: his hands were stained with blood, in peace as well as in war; and as soon as Clovis had dismissed a Synod of the Gallican Church, he calmly assassinated all the princes of the Merovingian race". Michelet continues with the important line, "He was then the only Catholic or orthodox king in Christendom, the other Christian kings being Arians, and his power was zealously supported by the bishops who reigned in the cities of Gaul". Paris became the capital of his kingdom about 507. The Goths or Visigoths viewed his rapid progress with jealousy and alarm, and some disputes arose on the edge of their contiguous dominions. At Paris Clovis declared to an assembly the pretence and the motive of a Gothic war.

> "It grieves me," he said, "to see that the Arians still possess the fairest portion of Gaul. Let us march against them with the aid of God, and having vanquished the heretics, we will possess and divide their fertile provinces." (Gibbon, in *The History Of The Decline And Fall Of The Roman Empire*)

Thus it was that Gaul became Catholic, and from thereon the story gets depressingly familiar – a story of heretic-burning under Western

Christian Emperors (Clovis was recognised as a Roman Consul in 510 by the Byzantine Emperor Anastasius). It is to Clovis and his successors that we owe the demise of Arianism (a form of Christianity readily compatible with truly monotheistic Islam, our 'enemy' for several centuries) and the rise of Catholicism – not to Constantine. It is from Gaul that Catholicism spread, not from Rome. The so-called missionary activity of the early Church was of the same kind; generally the barbarians were already Christians when the 'Romans' arrived and enforced Catholic orthodoxy. The Celtic Church in the British Isles was suppressed, and the library of the monastery at Bangor burnt by 'missionaries' who, our schoolteachers let us believe, came to convert pagans. Significant in this respect is the attitude of the Goths towards the Jews, who lived in Gothic kingdoms in France, Italy, and Spain, and who so much preferred these 'barbarians' to the neo-Romans as to assist with fanatical fervour in the defence of their home cities against Byzantine invasions. In Spain the Jews were accepted and made great contributions to the Gothic civilisation – until the coming of Catholicism. Anti-Semitic pogroms under the Catholics were endemic wherever their cancer reached, with the standard accusations of child murder and wicked idolatry as justification.

THE AEONOLOGY OF
RELIGIOUS DEVELOPMENT

If any form of paganism existed in the former Western Roman Empire, it was a paganism already undergoing transformation under a variety of influences. In the time of Julius Caesar, if not long before, the old state religion was finished. The movements we have described were flourishing, world-wide communications were effectively in place, and new religious movements were swiftly eroding the old and increasingly meaningless state religions of the Romano-Hellenistic world. From Britain to Syria one form of global civilisation was evolving, and the official cultus was simply inadequate and retrogressive. A new religion was needed for a new world – and the potent and civilising influence of Buddhism, with the salvationist cults of the Near East, together with the old Mystery religions of the Hellenistic world were the major ingredients in a melting pot of ideas. The revolutionary changes in the world-order had upset the mental and spiritual order of the ages. These exotic flowers flourished alongside the Messianist movement in Palestine; there were large Jewish communities in Syria and Alexandria also. The fate of all outside influences was to be interpreted via the two strands of Middle Eastern folklore (with its strong links to Judaism in its various forms) and Hellenistic philosophy (with its own equally strong links with the Gnosticising tendency). Once this process had commenced, any material, whether Buddhist, Essene, or Pagan, could be related to any other. Christianity is simply one such combination, with the marks of its crude adaptation to the needs of pro-Roman pseudo-history visible like the scars of carpentry on badly restored furniture.

This immense cultural phenomenon was utterly necessary according to the schema of Crowley's aeonology. It constitutes the overthrow of the 'Aeon of Isis', of dumb obedience to arbitrary Law, to superstition and empty ritualism. The price paid for this freedom was the 'Ancient Sorcery' in new form, the lie on which Western Civilisation was based, the body tortured by repression or persecution, the spirit enslaved in shackles of dogma and ignorance. That was the bitter end of the revolution of the human spirit that took place during the sunset of the Roman Empire, and a similar revolution may end as miserably in the sunset of that of the British. The Light of the Gnosis was also the Light of the Renaissance, with its deep indebtedness to the ancient world, including the Hermetic writings. This was the real emergence from the

Dark Ages of the 'Ancient Sorcery'. Perhaps, as Crowley occasionally believed, a five-hundred-year Dark Age will follow the magical flowering of his day, before a similar Renaissance of the Spirit truly inaugurates the Reign of the Crowned and Conquering Child.

Postscript

From: *A Short History of Sex-Worship* by H. Cutner. (Introductory Foreword by Maurice Canney, Emeritus Professor of Semitic Languages and Literatures in the University of Manchester!)

> There can be little doubt that the Bible contains many traces of phallic worship, though the uninitiated may find it very difficult to discover them. The Hebrew of the Old Testament is particularly difficult to translate, and it is certain that our English translators have glossed over many difficulties, sometimes in the interests of so-called decency. Even in the present 'original', as is admitted by C.D. Ginsburg [author of a valuable work on Kabbalah, from which Mathers unashamedly 'borrowed'. Ed.], one can trace the hand of the final editors who have tried to hide obvious phallic meanings to certain words. Most of the names of persons in the Bible are artificial. They each appear only once, as a rule, in the Old Testament. There

is only one Moses or Abraham or David or Solomon or Lot or Noah, and to understand these names is to understand a little how the Bible was composed.

The gods of ancient Israel were certainly many, and the people seemed to have excessive fondness for those indubitably connected with phallicism. Take, for example, Baal Peor (Numbers, xxv.3.). Baal or Bel means in Hebrew, as the orthodox Parkhurst says, ruler. Baal was certainly worshipped by many ancient nations, and belongs to the gods of the sun-myth. Peor, according to Parkhurst, means a wide, gaping mouth. According to Inman, it means the 'opening of the maiden's hymen.' Baal Peor may thus mean 'The Lord of the opening,' and the god later became identified with (or was) the god known as Priapus.

In spite of the fearful visitations of 'plague,' etc., the lamentations of Jeremiah, Ezekiel, Hosea, and other 'prophets' prove how difficult it was to wean the Jews from phallic worship. Even the great Solomon sinned in this way. The people insisted upon building images and groves upon high places. The 'images' were almost certainly phallic male, and the 'groves' phallic female. It is difficult to form any other opinion'.

The words Jacob and Esau have also an interesting significance. Inman considers that the struggle in their mother's womb was symbolical of the worshippers of the lingam differing from the worshippers of the yoni. Esau is preferred by his father, and is represented as being rough, hairy, and a great hunter. Jacob is preferred by his mother, and is shown soft, quiet, and a cook. The meaning attached to Esau is male; that to Jacob is female. As the later Jews were opposed to female deities, they changed the word Jacob to Israel.

Enough has been said, it is hoped, to show that though the Jewish nation after the fall of Jerusalem, and perhaps for a century or so before [sic], set their face dead against the 'gods' of the races surrounding them, and particularly against the 'abominations' of other religions, their own religion is full of their early beliefs; these were, surely, in many ways phallic. Whether this can or should be brought up against them it is for the reader to decide; it depends on the way one looks at the worship of sex in religion. From one point of view, nothing can be more degraded; from another, nothing can be more sublime.

www.ingramcontent.com/pod-product-compliance
Lightning Source LLC
LaVergne TN
LVHW051155080426
835508LV00021B/2634